Secret Place Poems

For Meditation and Inspiration

Nikki George

JT Publishing House

JT Publishing House

Secret Place Poems
Copyright © 2023 by Nikki George

Requests to the author for permission should be addressed to:
JT Publishing House, writing@jtpublishinghouse.com

Names: George, Nikki.
Title: Secret / Nikki George.
Description: Spartanburg : JT Publishing House, 2023. | Summary: "Secret Place Poems For Meditation and Inspiration are an invitation to still away from the busyness of life and meditate on scripture hidden within the poems. The poems uniquely interact with valuable themes such as identity, purpose, and our ability to surrender to God.
Many of the poems also take on a prophetic voice and can assist the reader in learning to hear and recognize the voice of God. Secret Place Poems can be spoken aloud as a decree or daily confession. Create greater intimacy with God as you engage in the poetic dialogue."-- Provided by publisher.
Identifiers: LCCN 2023937964 (print) | ISBN 978-1-954624-13-9 (paperback) | ISBN 978-1-954624-14-6 (ebook)
LC record available at https://lccn.loc.gov/2023937964

Disclaimer: Any internet addresses (websites, blogs, etc.) and telephone numbers in this book are offered as a resource. They are not intended in any way to be or imply an endorsement by JT Publishing House or the author, nor does JT Publishing House vouch for the content of these sites and numbers for the life of this book.

Published by JT Publishing, Spartanburg, South Carolina
www.jtpublishinghouse.com

Printed in the United States of America

10 9 8 7 6 5 4 3 2 1

Preface
Come to Me

Hear, Oh Israel, when I call
I'm calling to you; heed my call
Come to me weary and hurting
Destitute and lonely
Come to me, sinner and saint
Learn of my intimate ways
I speak, and the winds obey
I command armies, and locusts obey
I command the heavenlies

I AM HE; I AM HE
I AM HE that does all things
I AM the Master Healer
Bow down and worship me
Victory is in humility.

Table of Contents

Identity

Day 1
You are Valuable

You are valuable
And worth a great price
Because of the blood of Jesus
And His awesome sacrifice

Never see yourself
Through the eyes of man
The One up above
Has a greater plan

He has chosen you
From the foundation of time
You're beautifully crafted,
Hand-designed

God made you special,
You're fearfully and wonderfully made
Before the womb, God knew you
The workmanship He would create

You're so unique
You have your own set of prints
You're unlike any other
Now go and represent!

Reflect:

Does your self-value derive more from the opinions of the people around you or the God who created you?

Do you value yourself as an original design from the Creator?

Day 2
City Upon a Hill

You set me upon the cattle
And the ten thousand hills
To glorify your name
And fulfill your will

It was not by my power
Neither by my might
That you set me upon the hill
As a city giving forth light

Under the bushel
You said I couldn't remain
You placed me on the tabletop
And to all that look, I proclaim:

This is the Lord's doing
It is marvelous in my eyes
He turned my ashes into beauty
And set my feet on high

Reflect:

What is holding you back from being on display for God?

Do you have hidden gifts or talents?

Days 3
Queen

Scorn, mock
Say what you must,
I will not sway
But continually trust

In the Lord my God
The Creator of old
It will be Him
Crowning my head with gold

I am a princess
Who once walked in the night
Now my heavenly Father
Has turned on the light

Look, everyone
There's beauty to behold
You thought I was rubbish
But behold, I'm pure gold

Just like Queen Esther
I stand out of the crowd
The spirit of beauty
Now cries aloud

You cannot refuse
Or pretend you don't see
The royalty and splendor
God has given to me

Reflect:

Are you confident in who God made you?

Do you ascribe beauty more from internal or physical qualities?

Day 4
Unique

I am free
I am free
To be me
Unequivocally me

There's not another like me
I have gifts and talents
And things you might not see
But I am irrevocably me

You cannot change me
Rearrange me
And make me who you want me to be

God gave me splendor
Royalty
I'm a gem, you see

There's beauty to behold
There's loveliness untold
It's all wrapped up in this thing called me

I'm free; I'm free
Happy as can be

No longer bound
by what others see

I am a royal diadem
In the hand of my God
He created me
To show off
My prod - i - gy

Look at me, look at me
I like what I see
Oh yes,
I like what I see

Gifts inside
You cannot hide
You, too, are free to be

You are the lovely part of me
Dance, sing, write, and speak
Display your talents and be me
You are the essence of me

Love, praise, and kindness
Do good, have fun
Love others
That's who I be
I am irrevocably undeniably me

I have an attitude

That says I love you
No matter what you
Think about me

I am love,
That's who I be

I am love,
That's who I be

Reflect:

Is your identity found in what you do or who you are?

Are you being who God created you to be or who others expect you to be?

PURPOSE

Day 5
Purpose

Why do you think
That your life is your own?
God is the Creator
Have you not known

That He created you
Even before the womb
That your life would be His
Not yours to consume?

Die to your flesh
And totally commit
To carry your cross
And thus submit

To the Holy Spirit
As He gives unction
Showing you the direction
So that you may function

In the arena
You were assigned
And the purpose
For which you were designed

Reflect:

Are you able to define your purpose?

Was there a time in your life when you gave up your plan for your life to live God's plan for you?

Day 6
Sleeping Giant

Awake! Oh sleeping giant
Roar with a mighty roar
Let the light shine upon you
You're what I'm waiting for

Rise, oh, sleepy giant
To your rightful place
Far from discouragement
Far from a timid pace

Burst out with a vengeance
To punish the pain of before
Get up on your horse
And ride to Mount Rushmore

Amongst the noble and famous
Amongst the shakers of the world
Among those who realized dreams
And made complacency twirl

Reflect:

What will you do differently if you have areas of complacency that keep you from being all God created you to be?

Are you an overcomer?

Day 7
Write the Vision

Write the Vision
Make it plain
The written plan
Will sustain

The time of testing
The time of trial
When it appears
Not to be worthwhile

Follow your heart
Follow your dream
Let nothing stop you
Not even doubt's scream

Cast him down
And throw him out
And pick up the scroll
Let it lead you Now

Reflect:

What ideas or God-given dreams have you dismissed?

What goals have you written, and how are you working towards your dreams?

Day 8
Niche

I am the Lord
I will fill
By my Spirit
Will I reveal

Your little niche
The plan I have for you
Don't try to fight it,
Do as I say do

You are a chosen generation
A royal priesthood
He meant it for evil
But I'll use it for good

Trust in me
Trust and do not doubt
For I am the One
Who will bring about

The answer to
The thing you've prayed
Because from faith
You have not swayed

They may have laughed
And said you sound foolish
Now the laughing has ceased
Your faith overruled them

Reflect:

What makes you set apart from others?

Do you have a dream?

SOLUTIONS

Day 9
Jesus Will Fix It

Lacking in education?
I will make up for it
Lacking in dedication?
I will make up for it

Exceeding in procrastination?
I will make up for it
Devoid of alteration?
I will make up for it

By filling you with anticipation
Stirring up your imagination
Giving you a destination
Turning your life into a proclamation

Of Word-inspired meditation
Total fulfillment, no abbreviations
World looks on in fascination
Cup overflowing with impartations

Reflect:

Have you ever felt that you are not good enough?

Have you thought that it is too late for God to use you?

Day 10
I AM He

I AM He that causes life
I AM He; I AM He
The Good Shepherd
Who washed your feet

The words I've spoken
Have made you clean
I'm the Healer
Give thanks to me

I'm the redeemer
You are redeemed
Why don't you just follow me?

I lead and guide you into all truth
I'm the Good Shepherd
Who gives His life for you

I AM the inventor
Of witty things
I AM your Righteous King

Reflect:

How has God been a Good Shepherd to you?

How has God redeemed you?

FOCUS

Day 11
Another Voice

The battlefield
Of the Mind
Gives us the hardest time

When the opportunity
Comes to obey
We hear a strange voice say

That's not right
That's not God
The voice gets louder
An altruistic facade

Now that doesn't make sense
Says the voice
To live by what you don't see
Is such a foolish choice

You can not trust it, he says
You can't even figure it out
Why do you believe?
If I were you, I'd doubt

Reflect:

Where is the voice of doubt speaking loudest to you?

Have you ever taken a leap of faith? If so, how?

Day 12
Faith Meditation

Faith is the substance
Of the thing you can't see
It's real
Real as can be

It's the evidence
Of the thing you've hoped for
It's the evidence
Of the thing you can't see

Faith is the evidence
Of what you believe
It's the thing you've hoped for
The thing you can't see

In eternity is where it's real
Although you cannot see
It's real, so real
Real as eternity

Reflect:

What's the difference between hope and faith?

What do you envision happening by faith?

Day 13
What Do I Do?

What do you want, Master?
Am I in your will
Am I doing what's right
Am I being too still?

Am I seeking my own way
Am I leaning on and trusting in you
Am I supposed to teach
or am I supposed to sing

Am I supposed to direct
Am I supposed to lead
I know I can't do everything
What part do you have for me

Do I focus on family goals?
Do I keep writing what I know?
Do I help honey be a success?
Am I passing or failing tests?

Do I get a job,
Or work from home?
Do I start a business
Of my own?

So many questions
And so many paths to choose,
With your divine guidance
I cannot lose

Reflect:

Is God at the center of whatever you are doing in life?

Do you trust that God will guide you in your decisions?

RELATIONSHIP

Day 14
Never Very Far

Seek me
And I shall be found
Up high down low, wherever you go
I am still around

I will deliver you
Even from the pit of hell
Ask my servant Jonah
Who lived inside a whale

He sought my face
And to him, grace did abound
For shortly thereafter
Jonah was on dry ground

So no matter what you're going through
No matter where you are
Call on me, I'll answer you
I'm never very far

Reflect:

Have you ever been in a situation where there seemed to be no way out?

Have you ever experienced a miracle?

Day 15
The Chase

Speak to my heart
Let your voice ring clear
I'm drawing close to you
Father, please draw near

I'm hungry; I'm thirsty
My soul chases after thee
With all of my might
Lord, please choose me

I'm seeking, Master,
Ever so diligently
Reward my effort
By drawing near to me

Oh, that I might catch a glimpse
Of your glorious face
That would fill my soul with joy
And begin again the chase

Reflect:

In what ways are you chasing after God?

Are you satisfied with what God has given you?

Day 16
Relationship

Listen to my voice
Learn to obey
Seek me diligently
I'm the truth, the life, and the way

Fear not, my child
Hear my voice inside you
Follow the Good Shepherd
For I will surely guide you

Take heed of this moment,
Notice the hour
Speak by my Spirit
Be filled with my power

Hear and obey
Lean not to your own way
Let my Spirit guide you
Throughout your day

Reflect:

Has God ever spoken to your heart?

What do you hear God saying to you now?

Day 17
Seek Me

Seek first the Kingdom of God,
And His righteousness
Prove me now, says the Lord
I'm ready for the test

I said seek
And you shall find
The real thing
Not an idea of mankind

Come, taste, and see
That I Am truly God
Peel away the layers
Of worldly facade

You can't find me
Seeking your own way
Hear my Word
Trust and obey

Read the Bible
And you'll be liable
To see things
In a different way

Reflect:

Do you think the same way you did five years ago?

How has the way you think changed over the last five years?

Day 18
Follow

You hear my voice
Leading the way
Come closer
Just follow and obey

It's not hard
The answer is clear
I'm never far away
I am very near

You call on me
And I answer you
Giving you wisdom
So you know what to do

Don't delay
And don't doubt
Follow my words
They will bring you out

To that place
Of peace and rest
Promises fulfilled
Put my words to the test

Reflect:

What do you worry about most?

How easy is it for you to trust God?

Day 19
Churn

Keep the fire burning,
Keep seeking, keep learning
Meditate on the Word

Keep the Spirit churning,
Fasten your eyes,
But let the words keep rolling

Meditate on it in your mind,
Turn it over one more time,
Squeeze out its juice,
Let its fruit produce

Taste and see it's good,
Pass it out to the neighborhood
Drink it up and let it quench
Every dry place in a cinch,
Let it flow to the deepest place
Let it bring refreshment to your face

Pour it out and let it flow
Like moving waters, let it go
Throughout the Earth
Watch it gleam,

Watch it glisten

In the land,
Collecting others in a band
Let it burst upon the dams,
Till it flows into waterfalls

Reflect:

Will you stay motivated to grow spiritually?

Does your schedule allow a specific time to meditate?

SURRENDERING

Day 20
My Way

Come unto me
Trust and obey
Do it my way
See it my way

Not your own way
It leads to death
Come to a place
Of total rest

Cease from your labors,
Burdens and cares
Call on the Father
He is right there

You're seated in heavenly places
With Christ
Surrender your all
Give Him your life

You cannot do this
On your own
You must look to Him
Who is seated on the throne

Reflect:

What one thing do you believe God wants you to surrender?

Do you set aside one day a week to rest?

Day 21
You Say You Love Me

You say you love me
But won't do what I say
You said that I am Lord
But won't let me lead the way

My yoke, you haven't taken
My cross, you didn't bear
My words, you didn't listen
As though you didn't hear

You said you'd follow me,
Even until the end
Now you've forsaken me,
For your earthly fiend

Reflect:

How do you know you love God?

What pulls your time and attention away from God the most?

Day 22
Carnal Christian Repents

I am personally sorry
And truly repent
For not counting up the cost
Not seeking souls that are lost

For being fearful, not willing, and obedient
Full of pride and not of meekness
Double-minded and unstable
Relying on self instead of Creator

Lying to self and others
Weak and timid, unloving towards brothers
Looking back and seeking approval
Instead of steadfast and immovable

Not speaking the words you spoke,
Afraid to act, the Word was choked
Limiting you with a finite mind
Being gluttonous and a waster of time

Unsubmissive to your authority
Not drinking your blood, not in mode: Seek
Not putting on Christ, the cloak for sin
Not fully dressed, partial weapons

Murmuring and complaining
Your Spirit grieved
Lord I repent
For not taking heed

Casting your words behind
Like something common, not a rare find
For giving you part instead of the whole
For not letting you be in total control

For not possessing the land you gave
Through fear and unbelief, the promise fades
For not taking action when you said, "Go"
For moving slowly and blocking your flow

For being self-consumed, not mindful of
others
Walking right by hungry, thirsty, lost brothers
For not exposing the sin that was found
For keeping my shoes on, on Holy ground

For being stubborn and rebellious
And choosing my own way
Kicking against the goads
Snatching your yoke away

For not keeping your things in order
And allowing confusion to cross the borders
For not keeping first things first
For not having spiritual hunger and thirst

For not seeing and agreeing with what you
see
Calling unworthy your royalty
Not taking care of the temple you made
And the one without hands not properly
bathed

For not doing those things you placed on my
heart
And by omission, letting things fall apart

Lord, all of these sins, please forgive
Place it under the blood because I repent

Thank you for throwing them
In that forgetting sea
Thank you 1 John 1:9
For setting me free

Reflect:

Is there something you need to ask forgiveness for?

In what ways will you mature intentionally?

Day 23
Response

Father, Jesus, Holy Ghost
I know you have a deeper flow
Download to me what you want me to know

Okay, Lord, whatever you say goes
Send the rain to open the floodgates of heaven
River of water begin to flow
All eyes are upon you, God

Reflect:

Will you wait patiently for God to show you what He wants you to know?

Is there an area you need to say, God, not my will but yours be done?

Day 24
Mistreated

Let me hear angels singing
Let me see elders cast their crowns
Maybe I wouldn't be so high minded
Maybe I wouldn't frown

Or look down on others
When they do what is wrong
Maybe I would pray for them
Or lift them in song

Maybe I would worship
And remember from whence I came
Remember that I, too, was washed
And cleansed by His name

Maybe I'd grow patience
And maybe I'd mature
To see how much you suffered
And how much you endured

You didn't murmur
You didn't complain
You were treated poorly
But loved just the same

You weren't appreciated
For all that you gave
You were rejected
By the ones you came to save

It was not fair
Neither was it right
For the One who was so loving
To be treated with such spite

To be spit on and beat
To be mocked and disrespected
To be abandoned
To be denied and rejected

To cry out in agony
With no earthly companion
To first die inwardly
Pain beyond imagine

Great drops of blood
Poured out like sweat
All for those
Who didn't fully appreciate you yet

Reflect:

Has love or life required more of you than you thought you had to give?

How do you respond to those not valuing you or your sacrifice?

Day 25
Give Love

Love, love, love
Let it flow
You're not being taken advantage of
Let the pain of the past go

Give, give, give
All the love you have
I will replenish it
I'm a faithful Dad

Trust, trust, trust
Not in man but in me
Every hurt you'll ever feel
Trust that I will quickly heal

Obey, obey, obey
The scriptures
They tell you what to do
Unforgiveness is only killing you

Again, I say love
Love with all your might
It's the only way
To live the abundant life

Reflect:

Are you willing to let go of past hurts?

Will you run out of love if you give it away?

Day 26
I'm Calling You

I'm calling to you
Won't you hear my cry?
I'm asking you,
Please draw nigh

I'm knocking on the door of your heart
I'm leading you so you'll go far
I'm seeking you with all my heart
A Father's love has no start

I'm calling you to a secret place
I want to fill you with my grace
I want to bring joy to your soul
I want to honor you and make you known

I want to release a blessing on you
I want you to experience the truth
I want you to stand at my gates
Wait for me; I am The Way

You will always win
Defeating doubt and every sin
I conquered death, hell, grave
I am here to understand

I am here to wash your feet
I am here to give victory

Reflect:

Have you been afraid to answer God's call?

Can you recall a time where you felt like God was knocking on the door or your heart?

PRAISE & WORSHIP

Day 27
Praise

Praise me in the morning
And in the night
Hear the Spirit stirring
Turning on the light

Creating in you wisdom
To guide your every path
A supernatural strength
That gives you grace to last

Any test or trial
From deep within
Open up the vial
Of praise that never ends

Reflect:

How do you define praise?

What are the effects of praise in your life?

Day 28
Region

You are my King
You are my Lord
I will serve you
With one accord

In my heart
I pledge allegiance
You are my source
Covering every region

The region of love
The region of faith
The region of faithfulness
The region of grace

The region of peace
The region of compassion
The region of unity
The region of action

Reflect:

What region of your life do you need to turn over the reins?

What region of your life have you surrendered to God?

Day 29
Live Song

Let my life be a song so sweet
Giving you the glory
I will do what you ask me to
Giving you the praise

Let my life be a testimony
Giving you the glory
I will do what you ask me to
Giving you the praise

Ask of me, ask of me,
Let me fill you with my glory
I will do what you ask me to
Give me the praise

Let your life be a song so sweet
Giving me the glory
I will do what you ask me to
Give me the praise

Reflect:

In what ways are you a living testimony?

What will you thank God in advance for doing for you?

Day 30
Written Praise

God-inspired
And word-ordained
I will write every word
And bless His name

All that's inside me
Will lift Him up
God is so worthy
He fills my cup

With good things
And satisfied my mouth
He sits up high
Way above the clouds

Reflect:

Have you ever written God a note of thanks?

What are you most thankful for?

Day 31
Rearrange Me

Master, I love you
I offer my heart to you
Please don't leave me like I am

I cry out to you
Change as only you can do
Master, I cry out to you

Father change me
Only you can rearrange me
Make me be
Who you want

Father, I need you
Master, I heed you
Only you can change me

Father, come near me
Please, Master, hear me
I cry out to you
Only you can change me

Let your words rearrange me

I'm crying out to you
Lord, I need you
Father, help me heed you

Remember, I am man
Father, I need you
Help me to heed you
Remember, I was made from sand

Jesus, renew me
Let your life flow through me
But remember, I am only man

Until your Spirit fills me
I am empty
I can not do it
Not on my own

So Father, won't you help me?
Remember, when I'm empty
I need your Spirit
To fill me again

Only you can change me
Your Spirit constrains me
Only you can make the best of me

Father, I need you
Help me, Lord, to heed you
Help me to obey your commands

Father, I'm not worthy
Of the love you've shown me
Remember, I am man

Thank you for your love
Even when I had nothing
Jesus, you still loved me
Knowing I am man

You still forgave me
Your love still came to me
Jesus, you found me
Just the way I am

Now I feel so holy
Thank you, Lord, for showing me
Just whose I am

I am your child
You will never leave me
You'll never forsake me

You love me so tenderly
Just the way I am
Your love changes me

It makes me want to change
Your love is beautiful
There's nothing to rearrange

Your love is so perfect
I can only strive
To be like my Master
And look through heaven's eyes

I can only perceive
The Love you've shown to me
Now with my heart
I truly believe

That your love can change me
It can rearrange me
Your love is so lovely
You're everything to me

Reflect:

In what way has the love of God changed you?

In what ways have you grown?

Day 32
Worthy, Worthy, Worthy

Worthy, Worthy, Worthy
Is the Lamb who was slain
The Holy One of Israel
Jesus is His name

Worthy, Worthy, Worthy
Is the One who knew no sin
Worthy, Worthy, Worthy
Is the Savior of all men

Worthy, Worthy, Worthy
Is the One who went away
Leaving us a Comforter
Who abides everyday

Worthy, Worthy, Worthy
Is the One who conquered all
Death, hell, and the grave
Restoring Adam's fall

Worthy, Worthy, Worthy
Is Him that was cursed upon a tree
Bringing restoration

Becoming our High Priest

Worthy, Worthy, Worthy
Is the Word that was made flesh
Offering a perfect sacrifice
A priest, after the order of Melchizedek

Reflect:

Who is Melchizedek?

Why is God worthy of our praises?

SECRET PLACE

Day 33
Solitary Place

A solitary place,
Is where I gain strength
A solitary place apart
Is time well spent

A solitary place apart
Heals the brokenness within,
A solitary place apart
Turns bright a light that was dim
Making me one with Him

Reflect:

Do you feel recharged or empty after spending time alone?

Do you feel you have to fill quiet moments with conversation, noise, or other activities?

Day 34
A Sound

There is a sound
It's quiet and still
It's where I hear your voice
Telling me your will

There is a sound
When I'm quiet and still
The atmosphere is changed
And Glory fills the air

There is a sound
Of sweet and utter peace
Distractions are not there
And worry has ceased

There is a sound
Like a mighty rushing wind
Refreshing my soul
And reviving me again

Reflect:

How would you describe being in God's presence?

When are you most aware of God's presence?

Day 35
In Your Presence

There is a sound
I love to hear
It's in your presence

The sound of joy
A sweet release
in your presence

There is a sound
I love to hear
It's in your presence

It's the sound of one
It's the sound of peace
In your presence

It's the sound of love
The sound of victory
It's in your presence

The sound of One
A sweet relief
It's in your presence

There is a joy
It fills my soul
In your presence

Where worries cease
There's sweet release
In your presence

It's so much love
I can not hate
In your presence

There's so much joy
I can't be sad
In your presence

There is so much hope
There's victory
In your presence

There's victory
No enemies
In your presence

I know I win
When I'm in your presence

There's so much peace
There's no defeat
In your presence

No matter what I see
There's victory
In your presence

I cannot lose
I only win
In your presence

Oh what joy
Makes me complete
In your presence

There is a sound
I love to hear
It's in your presence

Reflect:

What makes you joyful?

How do you describe peace?

Day 36
New Births

What is this
Going on inside me?
I feel renewed
Life is flowing free

Rivers of living waters
Are gushing all around
The seed has been planted
It's deep in the ground

The roots go deeper
Into the heart of the Earth
Cataclysmically flowing
Ushering in multiple births

Reflect:

What scriptures talk about rivers of living waters?

What does "rivers of living water" mean?

WITNESS

Day 37
Minister, Minister

Listen
Let me give to you
The keys to the Kingdom
That's been promised to you

Whatever I say,
That shall you surely do
Your reward is in heaven
Where I will crown you

Look not to men
Nor study their faces
I've called you to speak
To all the dry places

So they might find rest
And Water for their soul
To never thirst again
For the wonder, they shall behold

Relect:

How does God use you to minister to others?

What are some keys that empower you in serving others?

Day 38
Witness

Give what you have
Let the oil flow

Seek after me
And it will show
That my hand is upon you,
And I've given you favor

Have love for me,
Lend to your neighbor
This is the way
You lend to the Lord

I will repay you
With more than before
Take my hand and
Let me lead

Let me guide you into peace
As you roam about the streets
As you go where I command
Take my sword into your hands

Let my words
Roll off your lips
Let your fingers point to this
Jesus, the way truth and life

Jesus, the sacrifice
Jesus, healer supreme
Jesus, who sets captives free

Relect:

Have you ever led a soul to Christ?

In what ways are you a witness to those around you?

Day 39
Heaven is Here

Heaven is here
Heaven is waiting

Where are the Sons of God?
Where are their manifestations?

Why does the heathen rage?
They don't seek my face
Neither do my children
Turn from their wicked ways

Where is the blessed assurance?
Believers falling, no endurance
Fight the good fight,
You will surely win

Fight til the finish
Begin again

Walk in my ways
Accept my statutes,
They tell you explicitly
What you must do

Comprehend with your mind,
Don't waste time
Fellowship with me
Let me lead you to Glory

A place where failure fades
A place of truth and grace
A place of victory
A place where captives retreat

A place where no wrong is done
A place that shines like the sun
A place where the Spirit calls
A place where mercy falls

A place where redemption reigns
A place where vision remains
A place where victors meet
A place of no defeat

A place where Glory roams
A place of a solid tree
A place of sweet relief

Reflect:

Do you see yourself as a son/ daughter of God?

What do you think heaven is like?

Day 40
Speak From Me

You are a voice for me
Speak to them what I speak
Hear from me and speak it out
Don't look for fame or clout

Humble yourself under my mighty hand
Let me train you how to stand
Guarded by my shield
Ready with weapons wield
Triumphant in battle array
Dressed to fight the warrior's way

Victory is in your mouth
Speak, declare, speak out loud, shout!
Victory is in your hands
Lift them high as I command

Give honor where honor is due
The King walks before you
Follow Him to the heavenly throne
Seek His plans, not your own

Honor Him in all you do
Let Him bring revelation to you

Walk before Him in honest ways
Let Him train you on what to say

Speak to the masses
Of heavenly love
Speak to the sinner
Like a dove

Reflect:

Has God given you a message to speak to others?

Will your God-given message be spoken from a place of love?

Day 41
Glory Revolution

I am sitting in your midst,
Talking and waiting,
But you resist
My arm outstretched
You push it away,
Not believing what I say
It didn't come in the package
You'd expected
So, it sits to the side
Seriously neglected

I call to you
But in a soft voice
However, the noise of the world
Was your first choice
I beckoned to you
And motioned with my hand
You walked right by
And followed your own demands

I pleaded with you on Sunday mornings
You rolled over and kept on snoring
You were tired

From chasing the curse
I have blessings
To quench your thirst
But you weren't thirsty
Didn't want my drink
Though I offered every morning
You weren't hungry
Because you had your thrill
You gorged on the world
And did your will

I offered you meat
The finest steak
You only wanted
Slow death on a plate

I tried to entice you
With my promises and love
You were content
Stuck in the mud
I reached out my hand
To pull you up
You wallowed around
In your own blood

I wanted to clean you
And give you a bath
But for my kindness
You gave me wrath
You blame me

For all your problems
And rejected the solutions
I offered to solve them
You have your own ideas
And follow your own ways
Now you're eating your own fruit
And don't like the taste

I had the choicest
Vines for you
I wanted the best
Wine for you
I would shelter you
In the best land
Clothe you in riches
Put rings on your hand
As my King and Priest
Why sit dejected
At satan's feet?

I made you to rule
Over all things
To multiply and
Speak like me
I made you to rule
And reign
I gave you
My DNA
Speak to the mountains
Make them move

Operate in my Kingdom
The Glory's in you

The Glory's in you
We have these treasures in earthen vessels
The glory's in you; go and tell them
The glory is here, and it's in you
Release the glory; I'm empowering you

Don't keep me inside and make me hide
Let me out; let the glory outside

The glory is here The glory is in you
You must release Him; He's in you

The words that I speak are spirit and life
Release the glory morning, noon, and night
Release the glory upon the Earth
Release the glory child of my birth

You are born again; release the glory, and let
others win
Release the Glory, clear the way
For the next realm of Glory coming today
The Glory is here
Do you hear what I say?
Release the Glory
Every Day
Release the Glory of the Lord
Let it fill the temple

Let it fill your houses
Let it fill your homes
Your communities, your streets
Your governments, your bathrooms,
Your places of business, your cars

Let the Glory of the Lord
Fill our nations

The Earth shall be full of the knowledge of
God
The Glory Revolution has begun!

Reflect:

Are you living beneath the blessings and privileges God has given you?

Will you release the Glory of God?

Day 42
Activate

I come to you with the finger of God
Take up your cross and walk with your rod
Performing my miracles for all to see
Wonder, Glory, Majesty

I glorify you as you glorify me
Take to heart the words I speak
Believe the word as you read
Seek for treasure found in me

Royal Diadem in the hand of God
Listen closely; don't go far
I AM the Master, and to you, I speak
Behold, I show you greater things
Wait on me and watch me show
Things to you, you didn't know

I will give you the upper hand
Believe in me, watch and pray
Let me deliver my message today

Reflect:

Will you write down what you believe God is saying to you?

Will you take to heart the Words that God speaks?

Day 43
Download

Send a download from on high
To open up spiritual eyes
Touch my Humanity
To think what you think

Let your light shine through
Sync my soul to you
Let me seek your face
Let me walk in your ways

Download abundant Grace
Send wisdom to save
Let me be the one
Connecting to your Son

Let me understand your words
Let your voice be clearly heard
Let your spirit thrive
Let it be my guide

Let faith arise
To heal blinded eyes
Let your glory appear
So the deaf can hear

Help me set the captives free
By your might and Majesty
Give me power in my tongue
To speak life to everyone

Download love to quench soul thirst
Fill me with compassion to heal soul dearth
Empower me to be your witness
Let mercy flow until everyone gets it.

Thank you for the download Lord.

Reflect:

Do you believe God has more to reveal to you?

Do you think receiving downloads from God will impact you and others?

Day 44
Marry Me

Take this journey with me
I'll never leave
I'm here on bended knee
Asking you to marry me

Be my bride
Be my wife
Let me give you
Joy inside

Let me whisper
In your ear
Will you hear?
Will you hear?

Reflect:

Will you trust God in the journey He is taking you?

Will you accept Jesus as your Lord and Savior?

Acknowledgments

Maurice George–you are my best kept secret.
I love you. Thank you for loving me and
supporting whatever hat I wear.

Nikki George

Nikki George is the author of *One God, One Message, One Day*, a 40-day devotional and *Speak It,* an inspiring children's book.

She has actively served in children's ministry for years and loves to help the younger generation develop their identity in Christ. George streams and hosts The "i" Witness Show with Nikki George. She is also the owner of NikkiNovelties and Write Company Publishing.

The University of North Carolina at Charlotte Alumna is also an ordained Minister and has been blessed to have 27 years of marriage. She and her husband Maurice are the parents of seven children and have two grandchildren.

Nikki's mission is to help turn the hearts of the children back to the Father and be a witness that spreads the gospel of Jesus Christ throughout the world.

<u>Follow Nikki online:</u>

Website + Email:
http://www.theiwitnessshow.org
theiwitnessshow@gmail.com

YouTube:
The iWitness Show with Nikki George

Facebook:
The"i"witnessshow with Nikki George

Instagram:
@theiwitnessshow